PRA
FOR

Also by Fay Sampson:

Prayers for Depression: And how best to live with it

PRAYERS
FOR DEMENTIA
And how to live well with it

FAY SAMPSON

DARTON·LONGMAN+TODD

First published in Great Britain in 2017 by
Darton, Longman and Todd Ltd
1 Spencer Court
140–142 Wandsworth High Street
London SW18 4JJ

ISBN 978-0-232-53297-5

A catalogue record for this book is available from the British
Library.

Designed and produced by Judy Linard
Printed and bound in Great Britain
by Bell and Bain, Glasgow

ABOUT THIS BOOK

Better health care means that many of us are living longer. This carries with it an increased probability that more of us will develop dementia, or will know someone who has.

The prayers in this book are divided into three groups. The first group is for the use of those with dementia. The second is for carers. And the final prayers are for the use of family, friends and the wider community. But you can use any of them with, or on behalf of, someone else.

You may wish to insert *him* or *her* or a personal name, in place of a more general term like *the one I love* or *the one living with dementia*.

The prayers are accompanied by information about dementia and the best way to handle its symptoms. It has not been possible to cover every aspect of this large subject. You may wish to add prayers of your own which relate to your particular experience. There is space at the end for you to do this. You may also wish to add notes about other resources you have found helpful to hand on to others.

'The Gate of the Year' is by Minnie Louise Haskins © Minnie Louise Haskins 1908. Reproduced by permission of Sheil Land Associates.

And remember that normal life doesn't come to a standstill when someone is diagnosed with dementia. Make the most of the time you have.

Half the royalties from this book will go to the Alzheimer's Society.

Underneath are the
everlasting arms.

Deuteronomy 33:27

PART A

For the use of, or on behalf of, those with dementia

'You know the way where I am going.'
Thomas said to him, 'Lord, we do not
know where you are going; how can we
know the way?'
Jesus said to him, 'I am the way,
and the truth and the life.'

John 14:4-6

Lord Jesus, hold my hand.

They tell me I have dementia, but that can't be true. All right, my memory is not what it used to be, but I'm as sane as anyone else. I'm not demented.

I've seen people with dementia. I'm not like that. Most of the time, I function perfectly well.

But the test results are in and they say that's what I have.

I'm frightened, Lord. It's not something I ever imagined happening to me. I fear the loss of my identity. I dread the falling away of what I know and can do. Put your arm around me as I journey into the unknown.

If it is true, then I am going to need help. Give me people around me who understand my anxiety about the path I must tread. May the light in your smile assure me of my continued worth in your eyes, just as you loved and valued me when I was a helpless baby. Affirm me in all that I am and have been, even if others see only my decline.

Are not five sparrows sold for two pennies?
And not one of them is forgotten before God.
Why, even the hairs of your head are all
numbered.
Fear not; you are of more value than
many sparrows.

Luke 12:6-7

Shepherd of my path,

so I have dementia. Give me grace to accept this as part of the pattern of my life and that of many others. May I enjoy the present moment and all the life I have yet to live.

Grant me the humility to accept the assistance I will need. I give you gratitude for all those I am finding who so readily offer that help.

Lord, you walked an unwelcome path you feared into a dark unknown. It took a greater courage than mine to do that willingly. In my darkening path, take me by the hand and share your courage with me.

And I said to the man who stood at
the gate of the year:
'Give me a light that I may tread safely
into the unknown.'
And he replied:
'Go out into the darkness and put your hand
into the Hand of God. That shall be to you
better than light and safer than a known way.'
So I went forth, and finding the Hand of God,
trod gladly into the night.
And He led me towards the hills and the
breaking of day in the lone East.

Minnie Louise Haskins

Patient God,

I don't mean to forget things. But I can tell from the exasperation in the voice that I must have asked this question many times. I know they are trying to be kind, but at times I feel like a scolded child. I want to feel valued.

The world is becoming increasingly unfamiliar to me. I know I used not to be like this. I used to be in charge of my own life. I didn't forget to take my medicines or change my clothes. It exasperates me that I can't remember how to do certain things. I forget the names of my family. It humiliates me. Frightens me.

Lord of the eternal years, I can't even remember what day of the week it is, but you have always known me, from the time I was in my mother's womb. You number every hair of my head. If I forget everything I ever knew, you will never forget me.

Anchor me, Lord, with the grip of your strong hand. When everything else is slipping away from me, hold me fast.

It feels like walking into a fog, but if you walk into the unknown with me, I shall never be lost.

Thou dost keep him in perfect peace whose
mind is stayed on thee,
because he trusts in thee.

Isaiah 26:3

God of Wisdom,

in a world which is becoming increasingly unfamiliar to me, it is an enormous relief to know that there are people who love me. People who don't give up on me when I appear foolish. People who make sure that I do the things I need to, who care for me, who take over the jobs I used to do. They give me a rock to hold on to.

I thank you that there are many other people around me who know that I have dementia and care about me. Doctors, nurses, support workers, volunteers, friends who stand by me. I don't always know what is happening to me, but they do. I give you praise that I am surrounded by so much love and help.

Most of all, your love enfolds me.

Can a woman forget her sucking child,
that she should have no compassion on the
son of her womb?
Even these may forget, yet I will never
forget you.

Isaiah 49:15

Faithful God,

my memory is not what it used to be. I forget things. I forget people. But they do not forget me.

I give you heartfelt thanks that I have people around me who love me and care for me. They understand what is happening to me.

Always I have you beside me.

You show me that it does not really matter if I forget things. I'm allowed to.

Give me the grace to see that the present is enough for me. I still have the sunrise on a frosty garden. I still enjoy my favourite food. I have not lost the gift of laughter. I have someone to guide me where I need to go.

And I have my memories of the past, which seem to grow more vivid day by day.

Let me meet the days ahead with trust and serenity. Bless all those who walk beside me.

Hold my hand.

You have been borne by me from
your birth,
carried from the womb;
even to your old age I am He,
and to grey hairs I will carry you.

Isaiah 46:3-4

Saviour Christ,

who knew what it was to be made humble and helpless, sometimes I rage against what is happening to me. It's not just that I forget things. I don't seem able to join in the way I used to. I get sidelined in conversation. I can't keep up with other people.

I feel they no longer trust me. They question whether I should be driving a car. They don't like me to go out alone in case I get lost. They keep telling me what to do, instead of leaving it to me.

I was once a respected member of my community. Now I feel like a little child.

Lord, can you make the people around me understand that I am still the person I was? The fact that I forget things hasn't altered that. I don't want to be brushed aside.

But you have known me since I was in my mother's womb. Even then, I was precious in your sight. I still am. You alone know who I am, and what is going on inside me.

Give me inner peace, though the world is becoming more troubling. Grant me your assurance that, in your eyes, I am and always will be loved, valued and cherished.

PART B

For the use of, or on behalf of, carers

SEEKING HELP

You notice that someone close to you is becoming increasingly forgetful. At first, you put it down to advancing years. Then gradually you realise that these lapses of memory can no longer be laughed off as 'senior moments'. A more serious change is happening to the one you love.

If this is dementia, then you know this change is going to be irreversible. The two of you are embarking on a journey that may be sad, bewildering, even scary. You would rather close your mind to it.

But take courage. You are not alone. A host of people are waiting to help you along this way. The sooner you and your loved one entrust yourselves to them, the better the outcome will be for both of you. There may be medication which can help. There is advice on living well with dementia. Don't miss this opportunity.

You will need to take the initiative. Encourage the one you are concerned for to report these memory problems to their doctor. Accompany them to reassure them.

You are likely to be referred to a specialist clinic. There will probably be a period of memory tests and possibly a brain scan before you get a firm diagnosis. This is precious time. Value each moment.

Guiding God,

your Son gathered tremendous reserves of courage in the wilderness to meet the road ahead. Let me have the courage to face up to the fact that we need professional help. Show me that true love lies, not in denial or false hopes, but in caring honesty. Let me be the one to realise that the best future for the one I love lies in facing up to this moment.

Reassure me that abundant help and support is waiting. First and foremost, there is the strength of your ever-loving arms. Then take us both by the hand and lead us to the place where practical help can start.

We have your gift of time still in front of us. Let us not waste a day of it by denying the truth.

We shall both need your bravery, your wisdom, your patience and understanding in the days to come. Bless us as we take the first uncertain steps into this new phase of our life.

THE WORD DEMENTIA

Cancer used to be the word that no one spoke. Now it is out there, upfront. Relatives and friends don pink ribbons, run marathons or shave their heads to raise funds for cancer care and research.

Yet there is still reluctance to say the word 'dementia'. It is part of the lingering stigma which still surrounds mental illness. It can be difficult for someone with dementia to accept the diagnosis. They may laugh it off as 'going gaga'. It may be easier to talk about 'memory loss' when persuading a loved one to seek help.

You will want to be tactful with the one who has dementia, but be honest with everyone else.

Dementia is as much a physical illness as cancer. Changes are happening to the brain and these affect behaviour and abilities. Someone who has dementia needs our understanding and help. Research into its causes and treatment also needs money, just as cancer research does.

There is a new movement to bring dementia upfront. People can sign up to become a 'dementia friend', and wear a badge to raise awareness. People with dementia are encouraged to carry a card to say so, so that they can ask for extra patience at the cash desk, or anywhere else where everyday tasks become confusing and they need more time.

So many people have dementia nowadays that it need no longer be seen as abnormal. Being honest about it, and spreading understanding is the best way to improve the quality of life for the one you love and for many others.

Truthful Christ,

you made your disciples face up to the hard facts they did not want to hear. Help me to meet this unwanted diagnosis of dementia in the same way I would any other illness. Give me the wisdom and tact I will need to help the one I love come to terms with this new word in our lives. May the arms of your love, and my own, be there to support and help them as they learn to accept this reality.

Grant me the openness to be one who seeks to change popular perceptions by accepting the word 'dementia' and speaking honestly about it. Through our lives, may I and the one I care for show others that this is a serious problem, but that there can still be much joyful life ahead for both of us.

With your grace, may I, and all the others in this situation, bring this word out of the shadows to be seen as part of the lives of very many people.

You never shrank back from telling the truth. May my honesty help others to accept and understand the reality of dementia.

UNDERSTANDING DEMENTIA

He was driving with his wife along the familiar road into town. Suddenly he exclaimed, 'I don't know where I am!' He pulled over to the side of the road and never drove again.

Dementia takes a variety of forms. One of the most common, Alzheimer's, is usually a steady decline. Its progress may be slowed by medication.

On the other hand, vascular dementia, another common type, typically proceeds in steps. The person who has it may remain on one level for some time, and then suffer an abrupt loss of ability without warning, like the car driver who suddenly found himself in an unfamiliar world. The condition may then plateau out before the next sudden decline.

There are other forms, like dementia with Lewy Bodies which may lead to hallucinations. A farmer watched a procession of tractors trundle along the hospital ward. Terry Pratchett had a rare form of dementia which allowed him to go on writing best-selling novels with a little help from his friends.

Someone with serious memory problems may be given a brain scan. This can help determine what sort of dementia it is.

Once you have a diagnosis, there is abundant help on hand to help you understand what is happening. You will be given literature to tell you more. You will probably be invited to attend classes where you will learn more about dementia and the best way to live with it. You will share experiences with others living with this condition and their carers. Some people find it hard to accept the diagnosis and react with fear. There is support to help them come to terms with it.

In the first shock of diagnosis, it is easy to back away and say, 'I don't want to think about it.' But love for the person you care for involves understanding as much about their condition as you can, so that you know how best you may help them.

God of Compassion,

you gave your time, your energy, to those in need. Grant me wisdom to understand more about what is happening to the one I love.

I give you thanks for the abundance of resources available to help those with dementia and their carers. I see your love in the professionals, the volunteers, the fund-raisers, the researchers. May I take with both hands the help that is offered to us.

Let me not be so bound up with my own problems that I neglect to give time, enthusiasm and money to increase the help available to us and to others. Show me how best I may support the efforts already being made. Make me an advocate for the greater understanding of dementia in the community. Help me to turn what is happening to us into a positive for us and others.

MEMORY

One of the earliest signs that the changes taking place may be dementia, and not just the increasing forgetfulness common in old age, is repeatedly asking the same question. It's the short term memory which goes first. Even when you know that it is due to physical deterioration of the brain, it can be exasperating. It can be hard to keep the impatience out of your voice as you answer the same question for the seventh time in as many minutes.

There is nothing that you or the one you love can do about this. You simply have to accept it as the new normality. You need to lower your expectations. It's not so irritating if you know this is going to happen. You simply learn to answer the question patiently, as often as it takes.

But there are things you can do to help. Don't burden the other person with more information than they need. It simply gives them more to worry about. Try to take life one step at a time. There is no need to discuss arrangements for what you are going to do tomorrow. It will only lead to a series of questions like: 'Where are we going?' 'What time is the train?' 'Who are we going to see?' each repeated multiple times. In your dealings with the other person, let tomorrow take care of itself.

Repeated questions may also be a sign of stress. Do everything you can to relieve them of anxiety about the thing that is worrying them.

Loving God,

you have been more patient with me and with humanity than we could ever expect or deserve. Grant me the same loving patience.

Let me view the failing memory with the same compassion as I would a greater difficulty in walking. Help me to be supportive, not demanding. School me to control my voice, so that I answer the seventh identical question as sympathetically as I did the first.

May I never be guilty of sounding as though this failure of memory is the fault of the one I love.

And when I fail, continue to be patient with me.

PREPARING FOR THE FUTURE

Most of us have a list of things we know we should do, but haven't got around to yet. A diagnosis of dementia brings a new urgency to this. People with dementia may function quite well at the moment, but the time will come when they no longer have the capacity to make legally binding decisions. It's important for them to get their affairs in order while they still can. And it's a good idea for their carer to do the same for themselves.

If you haven't already made a will, now is the time to do this, or to check if an existing will needs updating.

But dementia does not mean that death is imminent. The person with dementia may live on for decades. Yet their abilities will decline. Someone else will need to have the power to make decisions about their financial affairs and health management in the future.

Both the cared-for and the carer need to set up Lasting Powers of Attorney for financial and property affairs, and for health and welfare. You don't need a solicitor for this. Forms are available from the Office of the Public Guardian. They are simple and accompanied by useful advice.

You need to register yourself as a carer. There are support services available for people with dementia, but also for those who care for them. Carry the card in your wallet saying that you are a carer. If you have an accident, people will know that there is someone at home who is relying on you.

You will be encouraged to draw up an emergency plan. This will list family or friends who live nearby and who can step in to cover for you until longer-term plans can be made. The Rotary Club issues 'Message in a Bottle' capsules in which you keep a care plan for the one you look after. The recommended place to keep it is the fridge!

Now may be the time to think about where you live. Do you have a network of friends you can rely on? Would you rather be near other family members? Do you have access to public transport? It's a big decision to move house while the person with dementia is not too seriously affected. But if you are going to do it, it's best to get on with it. The longer you leave it, the harder it will be for the person you care for to come to terms with unfamiliar surroundings.

When all the practical provisions have been made, you can relax and get on with enjoying your lives.

Journeying God,

our lives have altered. There are so many things to think about, so much to come to terms with. Guide me to take the practical decisions that we must.

You know our weakness and our reluctance. We would like to pretend that we can go on living as we do now. It is hard to look into the future and acknowledge how much things must change. Be the Shepherd who leads us into the unknown. Let us do all that we can to ease that transition into a new way of life.

When we have done everything that we can think of, grant us the serenity to trust the rest to your hands.

LAUGHTER

Dementia is a progressive disease. There can be difficult times further down the line, but it's not going to happen overnight. In most cases, your partner or parent is likely to remain recognisably the person you love for years to come.

This time is precious. Make the most of it. Let it be as enjoyable for both of you as you can make it.

There may be things that both of you have always wanted to do. Can you still make that happen? Are there other things you can do together to store up happy memories and give a sense of well-being?

In time, the horizons will draw in. Travelling will become more difficult as the one with dementia becomes disorientated in unfamiliar surroundings. Yet you can still open the scrapbook of enjoyable memories from the past. You can revisit favourite places, invite old friends with whom you have shared the past, get out those photo albums or videos. Bring back as much pleasure as you can.

In spite of your loved one's declining abilities, you can still make the room ring with your shared laughter. Do it while you can.

God of Laughter,

I thank you that a diagnosis of dementia is not one of instant tragedy. I bless you for all the happy times we have shared in the past. Let me bring them to life again for the one I love. Let me create new days of enjoyment.

Give me the generosity of heart to invite others into our situation. Let the two of us show them that it is possible to live happily with dementia. Let them hear us laugh together.

Ever-patient Father, may forgetfulness and failings not be a cause for censure but for affectionate tolerance. We both have a lot of adjusting to do, but with your grace we can do this together.

You offer us boundless love. Let the one I care for be assured of my love and acceptance. Grant us many more good days together.

Laugh with us.

RELIVING THE PAST

One of the most helpful analogies I was given was of the memory as a bookcase. Imagine one shelf for each decade of someone's life, starting from the bottom. If an earthquake shakes the room, it is the books on the top shelf which will fall off first. Experience and skills learned early in life will last longest. A woman may forget something you told her five minutes ago, yet still be able to play whole piano sonatas from memory. A man who can no longer be trusted to catch a bus alone may yet remember how to drive a car safely, so long as there is someone to remind him where to go.

Don't underestimate someone just because they have dementia.

As time goes by, the memory of recent chapters in someone's life may fade, while they retain a vivid recall of childhood. When we were planning my mother-in-law's 80th birthday celebration she wanted to invite a cousin who had been a childhood friend. She added: 'And let's invite Harry's mother. It would be good to have some grown-ups there.' She had reverted to her 8-year-old self.

The boundaries between the present and the past fall away. Eventually, that person may truly believe they are living in that remembered past. Yet that past is very precious. People with dementia will each have had a uniquely interesting life. They have had skills, jobs, hobbies, relationships that are too important to be dismissed as 'living in the past'. These experiences have shaped the identity of that person.

It may be helpful to compile a memory file of photos and objects that recall the different stages of that person's life. It can be helpful too as a reminder of family, friends and colleagues they are beginning to forget.

For those going into a care home, it will be useful to provide an information file telling staff about the resident. The care staff may be surprised by their past achievements. It may change their attitude to a vague and shuffling elderly person.

God of Countless Years,
every moment of our lives is still fresh and precious in your heart.

Help me too to treasure our pasts. Let the need for care in the present day not blind me to the person they once were, May I be the one to unlock treasured memories. Help me to take the trouble to think what would enrich the recollections of the one I love.

May their present disability not lead me to treat them condescendingly. Inspire me to celebrate what has gone before and welcome them to relive what gives them pleasure and self-worth.

Give me the grace that I too may lay down a store of memories that will light the twilight of my old age. May walking in your way make mine a life richly lived and worth remembering.

RAPID ONSET DEMENTIA

Typically, dementia develops over a period of years. Carers and family have time to adjust and plan for the future.

But it is not the same for everyone. The onset can be sudden and the deterioration rapid. This is particularly hard for their partner. Before they know where they are, the one they love is in a nursing home, barely able to speak intelligibly and having difficulty walking. This no longer seems like the person they have shared their life with. There has been no time for that lingering, affectionate farewell that long-term carers are able to make. It is like a sudden bereavement.

There is no simple answer, no easy consolation. It does indeed need to be treated like a bereavement. The partner will need time to grieve for this unexpected and very real loss. Friends can accompany them on this journey, but they cannot fully share the pain.

All the grieving partner can do is to show the warmth of their love when they visit. Hold a hand. Talk, whether there is any response or not. Read a favourite poem, the sports page of a newspaper. Play music. We need to believe that our loving presence carries its own message.

You may find yourself withdrawing from your usual contacts. You can't bear the weight of sympathetic questions. If possible, allow yourself the support of one or two close friends. Let them filter news of your partner to the rest of your circle. Give yourself permission to talk to them about how you feel.

Above all, let taking it to God in prayer not be a clichéd response but a reality.

Dear God,

why me? Why do I see other people accompanying their loved ones on a long gentle journey, while I have the one I love torn from me so suddenly?

I don't understand what has happened to us. I wasn't prepared for this.

Am I being selfish? Did I think we two should be spared such pain in a world like this? I don't know what to think, only that I am hurting.

Give me the courage to lift my eyes and see those who have been truly bereaved. Let me understand more truly how much that hurt. Join my prayers, my tears to theirs.

Suffering Christ, you saw everything dear to you ripped away in Gethsemane. You, above all, understand what I am feeling.

Hold my hand and give me strength. May I go on holding the hand of the one dear to me and expressing my love no matter what.

May I lay my head on your shoulder and weep the tears I do not want to be seen by anyone else.

COMMUNITY

If you are caring for someone with dementia, the support of friends is invaluable. As the condition grows more severe, they will need to be accompanied wherever they go. They will become increasingly passive, and lose the incentive to seek out company for themselves.

You will be particularly fortunate if you belong to a church. Here you will have a caring community. There will be people, clergy and lay, who see befriending those in need as part of their vocation. They will visit on a regular basis. The church community will pray for you.

It is likely that someone with dementia will be able to attend church for years to come, and meet up with sympathetic friends. Some may offer to come and sit with that person, giving the carer a chance to get out alone or to meet up with friends. They may offer to take the friend with dementia out without their carer.

A network of friends can be enormously helpful. Yet former friends may withdraw, because they feel they won't know what to say. Those who once shared a common interest, like bridge or singing in a choir, may fade away as the one with dementia no longer keeps up that interest. The carer may need to take the initiative in inviting them to visit and revive these memories.

You may find it helpful to join a new group, which includes others in the same position. They may meet for coffee or tea and a chat. It may be a walking group with a not-too-demanding programme. Singing for the Brain does a great job of getting people together to enjoy making music, particularly songs which bring back memories. Music can stimulate people who are losing interest in the world around them.

There are groups just for carers. If you are feeling

lonely and burdened, it can help to meet up with others in a similar situation. You can compare notes, realise there are others who are having a harder time than you, exchange helpful information. Or simply free yourself to laugh at some of the things that happen.

Don't be too proud to admit that you need support.

Loving Christ,

you shared your burdens with your friends. Help me to cherish ours. May I not be afraid to show them how they can help.

You know how often I feel tired and overburdened. It can seem an effort to try a new group. Give me the wisdom to see that the one I am caring for needs whatever enrichment our community can provide to prolong the quality of life. Strengthen me with the courage, the energy, to seek out such friends, old and new. Grant me the humility to realise that I need not do it all by myself.

But you suffered the pain of friends who let you down. I struggle to forgive those friends who have dropped away because the one whose society they enjoyed now has dementia. Heal the pain to me and to the one I love. Grant me your compassion.

And thank you, caring Christ, that there is so much support for people like us. Give me the grace to accept it with open hands.

DEPENDENCE

One of their weekly pleasures is a pub lunch and a walk. He hands the menu to her. 'What would you like?' 'I'll have the fish,' she says. It's her favourite. 'What about you?' 'I'd like the curry,' he answers. 'Yes, I'll have that too,' she says. He protests, 'But you said you wanted the fish. You don't have to have the same as I do.' 'No, no.' She is becoming increasingly agitated. 'I'll have the curry.'

He wants her to be independent for as long as she can. But in a changing and bewildering world, he is her rock. She is afraid to make a different choice from his, in case she gets it wrong. It is better for him to accept this than to increase her anxiety by insisting that she sticks by her original choice.

It can be hard for him too, as increasingly the responsibility of choosing for both of them falls on his shoulders alone, and in more important ways than what to have for lunch.

It's sad too to see this person who was in charge of her own life losing faith in her ability to make decisions and do what would really please her.

Perhaps next week he'll forestall this situation by choosing the fish for himself.

As time goes by, she may well become dependent on him to the extent that she feels anxious if he is not around. It's important to build up a small circle of relief carers whom she knows well and trusts.

It can be hard for the carer to accept this situation and not try to force the other into making decisions. This will only lead to unnecessary anxiety. Your job is to smooth their path and give them as enjoyable a life as you can.

Lord, My Rock and My Salvation,

I need your help. Strengthen my shoulders to bear the responsibility that increasingly falls on me. Let me not be selfish in my choices. Make me sensitive to the other's preferences, so that I may choose for both of us what will give them greatest pleasure. Guard me from abusing the power they give me to have my own way.

You know there are times when I feel this burden lie heavily upon me, when I must take on tasks that formerly I left to my partner. Let me always feel your strong arms upholding me. You understand that I am finding it hard to be as strong as I need to be, that I am reaching a time of life when I would wish for fewer responsibilities, not more.

You astonish me with the courage you needed to take on responsibility for the whole world. Give me just a little of your bravery, your perseverance, to put my own burden in perspective.

May I never be too proud to ask for help, most of all for yours.

CONTENTED DEMENTIA

A daughter visited her father who had dementia. She was horrified to see him put the electric kettle on the hob. She scolded him about his dangerous behaviour. She feared he was becoming irrational. She demanded that he be sensible and live in the present.

But her father was not behaving irrationally. He was simply regressing into his past, which was now more real to him. He grew up in a family that didn't possess an electric kettle. You boiled water on the hob. He was behaving logically in terms of the world that he was now inhabiting.

It would have been better for that daughter to accept this past and take away the electric kettle.

When I first became a carer, I was recommended the book *Contented Dementia*, by Oliver James. The Alzheimer's Society has serious doubts about the rigid regime which has since developed from this. But there are still valuable things to be gathered from its general approach.

It's about giving the one you care for permission to live in the past when they reach the stage where it seems more familiar and reassuring than the present. Attempts to insist that they get real and stay in today's confusing world will only cause anxiety.

Someone may be drumming on the arm of his chair in an irritating way. But he may really be reliving his years as a musician. Rather than jolt him back to the present that has lost meaning for him, go along with that. Talk to him about those days. Make him feel good about himself. It is not unreality, simply an older reality. Why shouldn't he live in that, if that is where he feels confident and happy?

Carers and visitors can encourage and value this. A cricket bat, a garment lovingly knitted, a diploma certificate. These can reinforce the sense of worth, not of being laid on the shelf or treated as irrational.

Such souvenirs can unlock a flood of memories, lighting up the eyes of the person who once did such things. Living in the past can be a positive thing.

God of Many Gifts,

you value each of us far more than the wild flowers or the sparrows. You delight in those you have created. Help me to treasure the inner person of the one I love. Let me see beyond the veil of age and forgetfulness to remember them in their prime. If they regress so that they are reliving that past, then grant me the understanding to go along with that. Let me affirm what was important to them. Let me rejoice with them in past achievements and enjoyments. When I remember how much you value me, may I honour the whole person, and not just what they are today.

Give me the generosity of spirit to do all that I can to add richness to their remembered lives.

CHANGES

My mother-in-law regressed rather sweetly into childhood. She was happier being looked after in a care home, surrounded by people, than she had been living alone. Her sister, always a livelier character, became aggressive and had to be removed from a very nice residential home after she bit one of the attendants. Their father, usually a mild-mannered man, got his wife out of bed in the middle of the night and was found shouting at her in colourful sergeant-major fashion, as he drilled her with a broomstick over her shoulder.

We are each of us a unique individual. No one's experience of dementia is exactly the same as anyone else's. For some it is a gentle decline over many years. Others lose ability with alarming speed. In some, personality is affected more than with others.

Family and friends embark with them on a journey into the unknown. Where the change is rapid, it can be particularly hard for those who love that person to come to terms with it. These changes will have a profound effect on the life of the carer, as well as on the person living with dementia. The latter will no longer be able to manage things you relied on them doing in the past. At some point, they will lose the ability to drive. There will come a time when they cannot be trusted to go out alone.

It can be painful to see the one you have lived with for so much of your life slipping away from you. Eventually they may no longer recognise close family and friends. It can be particularly hard if they no longer recognise you.

But the person you love is still there inside. What there has been between you remains a reality, even if the two of you can no longer access it.

God of Our Ever-Changing World,

you are our one true stability. Take us both by the hand and lead us forward into this unknown. Let there be tenderness and understanding between us, even as the memories of one of us fades. Grant me the patient courage to face up to personality changes and still to go on loving.

I realise now more keenly than ever how much patience you have needed with humankind – with me, Lord. Let me give to another the unfailing love you have always shown to me, regardless of whether I responded to you.

Compassionate God, comfort my sense of loss as the one I love retreats beyond what I once knew. May they still feel by my presence how much I care for them. Accompany them with your light and love as they go into places where I cannot follow.

AGGRESSION

Some of the changes which dementia may bring are harder to cope with than others, both for the one with dementia and for their carers. Not everyone regresses sweetly into childhood. There can be personality changes. The person with dementia may become aggressive. A cousin's husband once threw her down the stairs.

This can be upsetting and even frightening.

Remember that the one behaving aggressively may themselves be frightened. Their world is becoming increasingly bewildering. They may have a need that they are unable to communicate and which is not being met.

Remain calm. Don't take it personally. Check for practical causes. Are they physically uncomfortable in some way? Are their glasses or hearing aids working properly? Has someone behaved inappropriately to them?

Don't rebuke them. They urgently need your love and reassurance. This can be especially hard if they have threatened you physically.

Above all, don't try to cope with this on your own. There are professionals who are used to handling this behaviour. There are volunteers on the end of a phone. Seek the emotional support of family and friends. Both of you need help and care.

Lord,
I'm in difficulty. For years, I've coped with memory loss in the one I love. I've done my best to keep them contented and assured of

my love. Now they shout at me and threaten me. I no longer recognise the relationship between us.

I know I should be praying for them. But I need help myself. I feel bewildered, confused and frightened too. Put your arms around me and reassure me. Hold me back from retaliating with angry words. Give me calmness and understanding.

It's a shock to be treated like this. Why would they behave like this to one who has loved them?

But you know more than I can ever see, still less experience. In your mercy, you love each of us unconditionally. You went to the Cross for both of us.

Heal the hurts this aggression causes to us. Give me, and others, wisdom to know what is upsetting the one I love.

If I can't take away the cause of this aggression, then give me the patience, the courage, the caring heart to continue giving the love I did before.

I thank you in your mercy that now, when I need it most, there are those I can call upon to help. Give me the humility to accept that I cannot cope with this on my own.

I certainly cannot cope with this without you.

MOVING ON

A friend of ours, whose wife had dementia, cared for her at home until both of them were in their nineties. She only moved into a care home for the last weeks of her life.

Most families want, or feel they ought to, care for the one they love as long as they can. But as the years go by the dementia is likely to be accompanied by other frailties of old age. Having dementia makes it harder to cope. It may cause difficult behaviour problems. If the carer is the same age, then they too will be feeling the effects of growing older.

It is a hard for a family to make the decision that the time has come for that loved person to move into a care home. It can feel like abdicating from a responsibility. We do not want to take the one we love away from all that is familiar to them. We fear that, however good and kind the staff are, they cannot love that person as we do. It feels selfish to acknowledge how much easier this will make our own lives.

The one living with dementia may have been in a care home for a short time to give their carer a break. It's a good way to test out possible future options. But it's a different matter to make that permanent decision.

Professional support workers may be better at judging that moment than family. It can be both hard and a relief to accede to their greater wisdom and experience. We will be saying goodbye to a large part of our lives. We fear we may not have made the right decision. We know in our heads that this has become necessary, but the relief is still shadowed by guilt.

Dear Christ,

you know what it is like to reach a crossroads in your life where you must make an irrevocable decision. You suffered the far greater agony of that in Gethsemane.

Look with compassion on me now. My fear is that the one I love will suffer if I make the wrong choice. I feel I should go on shouldering the burden. It seems wrong to accept the freedom and release of letting go.

Help me to see with clarity and wisdom what is truly in the best interests of the one I have cared for. Merciful Lord, grant me the humility to accept when I can no longer cope, when others can do it better. Take away the guilt and replace it with a grateful heart.

VISITING

There, it's done. The person I have cared for so long is now being looked after by other people. But the guilt doesn't go away. I wonder how they are adjusting. Are they happy, bored, well looked after? How much do they miss me?

The guilt doesn't end when you have decided to put a spouse or a parent into care. You try to assuage that guilt by visiting as often as you can. If it's a spouse or a long-term partner, you may feel you should visit every day. If you live further away, you will wonder how often you can and should make the journey.

The most common symptom of dementia is memory loss. Though you may be haunted by remembrance of the one who is no longer there, they themselves may not have such a clear memory of you. Since they do not know what day it is, they will have no idea when you last visited. Time has narrowed down to the present, or more likely the remembered past.

If your visits give them pleasure, then of course you will want to go as often as you can. You may be able to take them out. You can reminisce with them about things you both enjoyed. You can show them they are still loved. You can laugh with them.

But as time goes by, the link between you is likely to weaken. They may struggle to remember who you are. The things that once gave them pleasure may leave them unresponsive. You may sit there, holding their hand, even talking to them, without being sure that they know you are there.

It may be the staff at the care home who tell you gently that you really don't need to come every day. It won't make a difference if you miss occasionally, or if you come to leave longer spaces between your visits, if you stay for a shorter time.

You want to surround them with your love for as long as possible. Yet, as the one you love drifts away from you, you may need to give yourself permission to let them go.

God, to Whom the Shadows and the Light Are Both Alike,

take the one I love into your arms as they enter this dark valley. Accompany them where I no longer can.

I feel a sense of bereavement. It seems as though the one I care for is no longer there. I cannot know what it feels like, or how much they feel at all.

Grant me the healing of that loss. Give them peace. Give me peace. I let them go into your hands.

PART C

For the use of family, friends
and the wider community

FAMILY

In today's world, it is common for members of the same family to live a long distance apart. If a parent develops dementia this leads to anxiety for the children. There is greater urgency if that parent lives alone. Someone needs to be on hand to see that they look after themselves, that they live safely, and take their medication. There may be a neighbour or close friend who is prepared to keep an eye on them. A health worker may visit daily.

But the time will come when this is no longer enough. Then it's decision time. Should you invite your parent to live with you? This will be influenced by whether you have a spare room, whether you, and possibly your partner, are able to combine looking after your parent with your job commitments. If not, is one of you prepared, and financially able, to leave their job? Are there children involved?

What about the rest of the family? You will all need to ask yourselves the same questions. There can be tension if someone feels that others are not doing their share.

If your parent and you agree that a care home is the best option, should it be near you, or where they now live and where they may have a circle of supportive friends?

These are big decisions. The parent with dementia may be becoming increasingly dependent on other people to make choices for them. This puts a lot of responsibility on you and the rest of the family to find the solution that will ensure the greatest happiness for the one who cared for you when you were dependent.

You are not alone. Commit it to prayer. Seek the practical advice of those who are familiar with this situation.

Parenting God,

your Son was born in a stable, totally dependent on human parents. I now find my own parent in that state of dependence. I want to offer them the best future I can. This may mean sacrifices of my time, my freedom, my patience, my care. It may call for sacrifices from other people. Guide me with tact and wisdom as we discuss this together.

May my home be a place of loving welcome as long as my parent needs it.

Grant me the wise support of professionals who can see more clearly than I do what would be best.

If a care home is going to the best outcome, then help me choose that home with a view to their greatest happiness. May I involve my parent in that choice as much as I can.

Give all of us the wisdom to handle the financial decisions this will involve.

Loving Father, show me what is best, then give me the grace to embrace the decision we have made with warmth and loving humour.

I commit my increased responsibility to you. Give me grace to undertake this role reversal, to care for the one who cared for me. May the Spirit direct me and the rest of the family as we plan for my parent's future. May we listen for your voice and trust its wisdom.

THE OTHER PARENT

There are a set of decisions that need to be taken for a parent with dementia living alone. But if both parents are alive and still together, the situation is different. You will need to stand back a little and let the other parent make most of the choices. But that won't stop you feeling concerned. And the caring parent will need your support.

In most cases, your other parent will be able, and will probably want, to care for the one with dementia.

But both of them are getting older. It is likely that one or both of them has other health problems. The parent without dementia may already be feeling the need to ease their workload. Yet now they are having to take on tasks which previously fell to their spouse. Life will be harder, and lonelier.

If you live some distance away, it may be difficult to know what you can do to help. Certainly keep in touch more often than you used to. It will be a help for the caring parent to unload all the exasperations and inconveniences of living with someone with dementia, however much they love them. The parent with dementia may develop irritating habits, like losing keys or coats. They may neglect to take their medication. They may put things away where they can't be found. The carer may turn round in a crowded public space and find that their partner is missing. These may not be major disasters but they can take their toll. It helps to have someone to share this with, even if there is nothing you can do to change things.

If you live near enough, you can make more frequent visits to help out with those extra tasks. If you are further away, you may need to come and stay more often, even though that can be hard in a busy life. Give both of them pleasure with your presence when you can.

Only if you are in constant touch can you be sensitive to whether the time has come for the parent with dementia to move on into residential care. This can be a hard choice for the caring parent. You will need tact and wisdom to help shoulder this burden.

And of course, you will pray for them both daily.

God of Boundless Strength,

look with compassion on my parents who are struggling with this situation. Give me the grace to see what I can do to help, and to offer that help willingly.

May my carer parent know the certainty of your presence and strength. Give them wisdom to make the choices that will be best for both of them. May your loving Spirit fill the change in their relationship. Comfort that sense of bereavement.

I trust you to hold the hand of my parent with dementia. I can imagine only a little of what it feels like to be entering that mental fog. Assure them how much I love and value them. Help me to cherish the past we shared and bring it to mind for their enjoyment. Let me make the happiness of both of them my priority.

Let me be a rock when they need it. Let me awaken laughter when things are getting them down. May they know that I will always be there for them, as you are always here for me.

FRIENDS

In today's ageing population, more of us are finding that we know someone with dementia.

What can we do? If we have not had close experience of dementia, we may feel hesitant about communicating with someone in that situation. What do we say? What help would be welcome?

Dementia is usually a slow decline. For some time to come, the person who has it will still be able to converse normally to a large degree. But don't expect them to make the sort of contributions they used to. You will need to take the initiative.

They will have trouble remembering what they did five minutes ago. But if you touch on memories from the past, your friend is more likely to respond. They may have forgotten what happened this morning, but have a vivid recall of their younger days. There may be experiences the two of you shared which you can use.

If you haven't seen that person for a while, it may be a good idea to show them pictures of friends and family. Older photos may work particularly well. But offer all this as a gift, not something to be traded in an effort to stimulate a response. If you get one, take it up gladly. Yet remember that your only aim is to make this encounter an enjoyable experience for both of you.

You will feel sympathy for their carer, yet wonder what you can do to help. As it becomes increasingly difficult for the cared-for one to be left alone, you could offer to come and sit with them, or take them out. Looking after someone with dementia can be tiring and isolating. The carer needs to have time on their own or the chance to meet up with friends. You can make that possible.

Do all you can to make both of them feel that they

are still valued members of your community. Don't back away when they need you.

Hold them in your prayers.

Friend of the Friendless,
when I look around me, I see a number of friends and acquaintances with dementia. It is tempting to look away and tell myself it is somebody else's problem.

Shepherding Christ, you went out of your way to find the lonely and the lost. Grant me compassion and insight to feel what it is like for someone who is losing their memory, increasingly adrift in a once familiar world. Let me be the one to hold out a hand that can anchor them to the life and friendships they knew.

Grant me the wisdom to see how I can help their carer, and the will and energy to act on that knowledge. Let me not make excuses. Save me from being the one who passes by on the other side of the road.

Lord, you were always ready to speak out for those in need. Guide me to find out more about dementia. Give me the commitment to be a Dementia Friend, and to advocate greater understanding in the community.

May I have your courage not to back away from the unfamiliar, but to reach out the hand of love.

QUESTIONS

If you live with someone with dementia, then you learn what works with them and what to avoid. But what if you can visit only occasionally, or meet an old friend once a week?

The thing is not to make your conversation too demanding. A polite generality, like 'How are you?' may be OK. You're not really expecting a detailed answer. But avoid direct questions about what the other person has done or is going to do. 'What are you doing for Christmas?' may be met with a blank stare or a look of panicked confusion. Better to chat about what you are doing.

Normal conversations proceed by one person asking a question, the other answering and then asking a question of their own. The conversation goes to and fro, like two tennis players having a knock-up over the net.

But asking questions of someone with dementia can lead to anxiety. They feel they should know the answers to these questions, but the memory eludes them. This lowers their self-esteem.

We need to change our usual approach. Instead of asking questions, talk about subjects that once meant something to that person. Recall shared experiences, news about family members or friends. This may trigger memories from the past, but don't demand them.

It is hard for someone with dementia to hang on to the information they already have. This makes them unlikely to ask questions to find out more about you. You will need to make most of the running.

My Lord and My Friend,

guide me with tact and wisdom to enrich my encounters with my friend with dementia. May I not be scared off by the fear that I won't know what to say. Fill me with your certainty that this is still the person I knew and valued. They may have forgotten our times together, or even forgotten me, but, if you will, use me to rekindle the warmth of our past.

I will need your imagination, your patience. Show me how to unlock the memories of the experiences and the people we shared. Give me the grace not to feel rejected if I get little response. Let me still be an enjoyable storyteller and companion.

As you have befriended me through thick and thin, may I make my friend feel valued by my willingness to share my time and enthusiasm with them. Give me the generosity to include them in our community in whatever way I can.

Be my faithful friend as I seek to befriend the other.

ADAPTING

Dementia typically creeps up on someone gradually. There can be exceptions: for instance, when it is brought on by a stroke. More typically, it may be some while down the line before anyone uses the word 'dementia'. The first symptom is likely to be forgetfulness, but that can happen to many older people without dementia being the cause. A stronger indication is repeatedly asking the same question. Friends will notice that something is changing.

The person concerned may speak light-heartedly about 'going gaga' or 'losing my marbles'. At this stage they should still be able to hold a lively conversation with you.

As time goes by, things become more confused for that person. You will notice a greater vagueness, a difficulty in picking up on things you mention which used to be familiar to you both.

It is now that you need to reach out a hand to guide them through that fog. Without being patronising, keep your conversation simple. Speak more slowly. Give them time to take in what you are saying. Talk in shorter sentences. Don't give them too much information to take in at one time. Offer helpful clues about the people or things you are referring to, such as 'My daughter Karen', rather than just 'Karen'.

When you are in a group, you are likely to find that the one with dementia withdraws from the conversation. They find it too hard to keep up with the rest of you. Reach out with warmth to include them. You may turn to them and say, 'Do you remember when…?' But not in a challenging way which demands an answer. You are simply making them feel they are still included in your group. Steer the conversation to topics they can relate to.

Increasingly, the past will become more vivid to them than the present. Use that.

As the condition develops, your friend may no longer socialise in the places where you used to meet. Don't give up on that friendship. Go and visit them.

In time, conversation will become harder work. You may not be sure how much your friend is aware of your presence. Don't be discouraged and abandon them. Let them feel in the warmth of your voice how much you still value them. Let them know they are loved.

Ever-Loving Lord,

I live secure in the knowledge that you will never leave me. Fill my own heart with loving constancy, so that I may be a true and lasting friend. Whatever the changes, may I accompany the one who needs me for as long as it takes.

Give me the Spirit of wisdom. Let my caring conversation take account of my friend's failing capability. Guide me to bring warmth and laughter into that situation. May our meetings bring them happiness and a feeling of worth.

Forgive me for the times when I have neglected a friend in need. Grant me your compassion, your constancy.

THE CHURCH

Most of us know someone with dementia, either closely or at a distance. It is likely that there will be several in your church. Naturally, we feel sympathy for them and for their carer, but we may not know what we can do beyond praying for them.

The important thing is to make them feel that they are fully valued as members of your community. Go out of your way to welcome them, before or after the service.

Include them in group conversations, without putting too much pressure on them to contribute.

Don't sideline them. Activities in the church may be just what they need to give them a full and happy life as long as possible. If they seem to be dropping out, give them a special invitation to an activity. Perhaps offer to pick them up.

Don't underestimate their abilities. If they used to read the lesson, they may still be able to do it well. It just needs someone to cue them in, so that they are not anxious about when to go to the front. Praise them afterwards. You could ask them to hand out books and service sheets, to move chairs, to wash coffee cups. Use your imagination.

Now is the time when it may be helpful for them to join in things they didn't before: a daytime fellowship meeting, a lunch club. Think about what your church can offer. Could you extend this invitation to those beyond your congregation?

Over time, those with dementia will become less active. You may see them less often in church. Perhaps a group of you could get together and draw up a rota for weekly visits. Don't just leave it to the clergy and pastoral visitors.

If they do not have transport, or have had to give up driving, take them out occasionally. As they become more disorientated, find out their favourite, familiar places and awaken happy memories by taking them there.

Don't let them be relegated to the list of the housebound you pray for but never visit.

As a church community, find out what you can do to make your church more dementia friendly.

God who has made the Church one Family,

you went out of your way to include those on the edges of society. May our doors and our hearts be open to all. Grant us the insight to see when one of our members is increasingly in need of help. Let us be quick to ask what we can do, and faithful in offering that support.

Give us the wisdom to see the person with dementia as you see them: as a unique individual, valued and loved. Let us not write them off because they have a disability. Show us the many ways in which they can still be part of our community, the avenues of service still open to them. Guide us to show them new ways in which they can be valued.

It's easy to overlook them. May we make time in our busy lives to include them and assure them of our continued love.

Save us from leaving the care of those with dementia to the clergy and pastoral visitors. Teach us to be a dementia friendly church.

SPREADING THE WORD

Like cancer, dementia used to be a word people were afraid to speak. Ignorance led to fear of the condition itself. It carried a stigma, as many mental health conditions still do.

Greater understanding has changed that. We now know that dementia is a consequence of physical changes in the brain. A brain scan can tell health professionals what is happening.

As yet, there is no cure for dementia, not even a way of halting its progress. Medication may slow the development of Alzheimer's, but not reverse it.

That does not mean there is nothing we can do. Greater knowledge of the condition, and the way it is likely to develop, means that we can adapt our behaviour to help. We can modify our conversation to make it easier for the other. We can use regression into the past to awaken pleasurable memories. We can avoid putting that person into situations which will cause anxiety.

Instead of seeking to hide the diagnosis from others, the more people that know about it the better, as long as they know what they can do to help. Dementia can make it difficult for people to handle the payment of purchases. They may be confused about how much money to hand over, or struggle to remember their pin number. Those in business have long been made aware of how they can assist those who are deaf, blind or have mobility problems. Increasingly, they need to recognise and understand the needs of people with dementia and how best to help them.

We can be ambassadors for them. The more we talk about dementia, and the sort of assistance people need, the greater likelihood there will be that they are met with sympathy and help. You can register as a Dementia Friend.

The Alzheimer's Society does splendid work in offering assistance to those with dementia and their carers. Despite its name, it covers all types of dementia. It offers a host of resources and information. It runs classes and support groups. It offers advice on the end of a telephone. You can get involved to make their work more widely known and support them.

God of Truth and Compassion,

your heart reached out to those who were stigmatised. Stir up in me the spirit to reach out to those who do not yet understand dementia. Make me instrumental in taking away the fear and stigma of the word.

May I give my willing support to those who work for greater knowledge of, and effective treatment for, dementia. May I be your instrument in making it a higher priority for a society in which ageing brings many more cases year by year.

In your compassion, let me comfort those who react with fear and dismay to the diagnosis. May my reaction show them that dementia is not unmitigated tragedy. May I encourage them with the assurance that there can still be years of enjoyable life ahead, and loving care in the final years. Give me the grace to change attitudes in those I meet.

RESOURCES

There is a great deal of help and support available for those with dementia and their carers.

When someone is diagnosed with dementia, they and their carer will be given details about the services in their area. There will be booklets, classes, support groups. A dementia support worker will be on the end of the phone. There will also be health checks and other support for carers.

Alzheimer's Society. Their website is full of helpful information. They deal with all kinds of dementia, not just Alzheimer's. www.alzheimers.org.uk. Alzheimer's Society, Devon House, 58 St Katharine's Way, London E1W 1LB

Age UK. www.ageuk.org.uk/Dementia Help. Tavis House, 1-6 Tavistock Square, London WC1H 9NA.

Singing for the Brain. Information about local groups can be found from the Alzheimer's Society.

Contented Dementia. Oliver James (Vermilion).

Bible quotations are from the Revised Standard Version.

My grateful thanks to those who have read this book and made helpful suggestions, particularly Jack Priestley, Margaret Farrow, Paula Baker. I am indebted to the many people who have shared their experiences with me. My gratitude to the NHS, the Alzheimer's Society and to all those, professionals, volunteers and friends, who have given generous help in my own situation.

These pages are left blank for your own prayers.